Introduction

"He is a gentleman; I am a gentleman's daughter; so far we are equal," Elizabeth Bennet stated to Lady Catherine de Bourgh in Jane Austen's novel *Pride and Prejudice*.[1] But what did it mean to be a gentleman in Jane Austen's England? How did a gentleman conduct himself? Men like Mr. Darcy and Mr. Knightly, born to wealth and privilege as members of the gentry, were trained from infancy on how to be a gentleman. Wealthy families like the Darcys and the Knightleys hired the best tutors and dancing masters to instruct their sons on proper etiquette and the deportment expected from members of the gentry class. Their education would have been refined at boarding schools and at Cambridge or Oxford University.

This was the world in which Jane Austen was born into and wrote about in her novels. But times were starting to change, and with the rise of manufacturing and trade a new breed of gentlemen were entering the rarefied world of the gentry. These self-made gentlemen earned their position in the gentry through hard work, military exploits, and advantageous marriages. As youths they did not have the advantages of a tutor or dancing master to learn how to behave as gentlemanlike manner. To aide these self-made men, books such as *A System of Etiquette* by the Reverend Dr. John Trusler were produced to guide young men on the proper etiquette of their class.

---

[1] Jane Austen, *Pride and Prejudice*, (London: Penguin Books, 2003), 337.

John Trusler wrote from experience. Born in London in 1765, Trusler's father ran a tea garden in Marylebone. His father's economic success allowed Trusler to be sent to Westminster School before being admitted to Mr. Fountaine's seminary. Trusler completed his education at Emmanuel College, Cambridge, where he graduated in 1757. Returning to London, Trusler translated Italian burlettas into English and adapted them for the stage. This career was not finically lucrative and to support his wife, Trusler took holy orders in 1759. In 1769, Trusler became a publisher, bookseller, and writer. Trusler wrote several etiquette books, including *A System of Etiquette* which was published in 1804. With the profits from his bookshop, Trusler was able to purchase an estate at Englefield Green, Middlesex. Trusler died in 1820 in Bath, England.[2]

I found *A System of Etiquette* to be a delightful glimpse into the world of Jane Austen and her characters. Through Trusler's book, I have gained a greater understanding of the world Austen wrote about. The book serves as a time capsule to a vanished world. Though published two centuries ago, I still found some of Trusler's suggestions to be particularly powerful in a modern world where etiquette and deportment has largely been forgotten. I hope that my readers will find the same delight that I found while pursuing the following pages.

Note: I have retained the original spelling and punctuation throughout the text.

---

[2] https://en.wikipedia.org/John_Trusler.

Advertisement

The following letter has given rise to the ensuing pages.

Rev. Dr.

Knowing the readiness with which you attend to the wants of mankind, from the many useful publications, to which you have already given birth, permit a youthful stranger, unversed in the ways of the world, yet wishing to live upon amicable terms with it, and which is not to be done without great experience and attention to the forms of society, to suggest to you the idea of composing a whole "System of Etiquette;" *to guide the novice thro' the intricacies of polite life, to direct him wherein he is to give and take place; how he is to regulate his visits, calls and notes of enquiries; how he is to conduct his correspondence, and how to subscribe himself, and direct to others, illustrated by cases and examples— and a benevolent heart may, do much in preventing quarrels, and in regulating, and combating the horrid practice of dueling.*

From your humble Servant,

and obliged

URBANUS.

To the Rev. John Trusler.

A System Of Etiquette

HAVING published *The Principles of Politeness*,[3] and the Art of living in the World, I should conceive that I had done sufficient to introduce a young man into life, but I find there is one knowledge still to teach, namely *Etiquette*, or those forms of Society necessary to be known by every young gentleman who wishes to be well received, and which is not to be learned without some general rules to instruct him. To this end, that nothing may be wanting on my part, who have already taken some pains to form the young man of fashion, I will at the desire of my correspondent give him what I call *A System of Etiquette*.

There is no living well in society without submitting to, and falling in with, the forms of it, absurd as many of them may be— but fashion is absurd in most of its modes.

These forms differ in different countries, but we have nothing to with any but our own, and I trust the following hints will answer all the purposes designed.

I will first enter into that conduct necessary to be observed in our intercourse with our acquaintance, and next into that respecting our dealings with the world.

In *The Principles of Politeness*, I have touched on many things that will naturally occur on the subject before us. That work

---

[3] *The Principles of Politeness, and of Knowing the World by the Late Lord Chesterfield* by John Trusler (1798).

is abroad in the hands of thousands, and I must refer to that book, rather than repeat the contents of if here. Some few of the more necessary parts I will add by way of notes: the book has gone through sixteen editions, the best proof of the public estimation it has to boast of.

The first thing necessary to be here noticed is,

Mauvaise Honte.[4]

Mauvaise Honte is that awkward bashfulness we perceive in young people (and indeed in many old ones) when they appear in the presence of those whom they conceive to be in a more exalted sphere of life than themselves. The French have distinguished this by the appellation of a wrong, or ill-judged shamefacedness, which term we have adopted.

Every young gentleman, when arrived at manhood, if he is a gentleman by birth, by fortune, by profession, or education if he has done nothing to degrade himself, is fit company for a prince, and this *mauvaise honte* arises from his not having a consciousness of it.

Glover,[5] the celebrated dancing master, who about 50 years since, taught most of our young men of fashion; in order to inspire them with courage and dignity, told them, when dancing a minuet, always to consider themselves as princes. So it is necessary for a young gentleman to be conscious that in point of rank he is equal to the most exalted personage he approaches; for it matters not,

---

[4] French term for "false shame, false modesty, painful shyness."

[5] A Mr. Glover was listed as the dancing master for Princess Amelia (1711-1786) in 1761 for which he was paid £240 in *The Universal Scots Almanack: For the Year of Our Lord, M.DCC.LXI.*

whether a man possesses 5000*l.* a year or 500*l.* if he is truly a gentleman; a prince can be no more.

Fortune will make some difference with respect to dinner-visits, but as to visits of ceremony, all gentlemen are on a par. If a young gentleman is unmarried, or does not keep house, invitations to dinner or supper are not expected, in return for any civilities of the like kind he may have received; nor in point of making entertainments, can a man of 500*l* a year, expect to vie with one of 5000*l.* Indeed, men accustomed to a great stile [style] of living at home, are not very ready to accept invitations to dinners or suppers, at houses where they cannot be equally well entertained; but from young gentlemen who are not family-men such entertainments are not looked for. If they bear an equal part of the expences at any public entertainment, it is all they need do; and where such expences are likely to be more than they can afford to enter into, they have only politely to decline the engagement.

In all other cases, one gentleman is on par with another, and while he can dress well, and make as good an appearance abroad, there is no cause for bashfulness or timidity, "The man who is ignorant of his own merits, is no less a fool, than he who is constantly displaying it." If bashfulness will obtrude itself at first, it will soon wear off, and the young stranger will acquire that confidence in himself, that is necessary for his happiness.

Respect To Superiors, &C

But in learning what is due to ourselves, we must not forget what is owing to others.

There is a respect due to our superiors, which a real gentleman never fails to shew, and that upon all occasions. By superiors, I mean men of greater rank, men advanced in life, or of superior knowledge. Fortune is supposed to give a man precedency, but I think erroneously; but if others do it where we are, *we* should.

If you meet an *acquaintance* of this character, either in your walks, or your rides, it is your place to make the first salute; and if going the same way, either to accompany him or not, as you find it most agreeable to him, and not leave him at any time (unless engagements call you) whilst he seems disposed to hold converse with you. It is a proper mark of respect to give him the wall if walking, and to break way for him; should he be on foot and you on horseback, there cannot be a stronger test of politeness, or greater mark of respect, than instantly alighting, giving your horse to your servant, if you have one, and accompanying him on foot, (this is, provided you are both going the same way) if you have no servant with you, lead your horse by the bridle if he will lead, or make an apology for not alighting, if alone, and your horse is untractable. This polite attention is more particularly due to ladies, and a man is a blockhead, if he omits to pay it.

The general salute of persons passing one another in carriages, is merely letting down the side glass and bowing.

Should you, either riding or walking, pass a person much your superior in rank, it is your place to bow to him, not to stop or accost him; but should he stop or accost you, it is your place respectfully to attend to it.

If you ride in company with a superior, keep to the left of him, where the road will admit it; if not, drop behind and keep far enough back, if the lane be miry, not to splash him with your horse; if you pass through a gateway, permit him to pass first.

In driving (tho' apart from etiquette, it may not be unuseful to know, that) it is invariably the rule where it can be done, to keep the left side of the road; by so doing, carriages never meet, so as to obstruct each other; according to the old doggerel verse:—

The rule of road is a paradox quite,

For, as you are trav'ling along,

If you keep to the left, you are sure to be right,

If you keep to the right, you'll be wrong.

If in company with a superior, whether walking or riding, should you meet an acquaintance of lower degree, do not stop to speak to him, but salute him only as you pass.*

*On paying a visit to a superior, if admitted, it is not respectful to enter his apartment, if you can help it, in dirty shoes, or a great coat; take off your surtout[6] before you enter, and leave it, with your hat, cane, and gloves, if you visit is to be any length, in the ante-chamber; but if it be merely a visit of respect, or on business that requires but a short stay, if you wear gloves keep them on, and your hat and cane in hand.

If a servant is in the way, wait to be introduced, if not, knock at the chamber door gently, and when admitted, or desired to sit, seat

---

[6] An over-frock coat worn by cavalry officers in the 18th-century to the early 19th-century.

yourself, but not in a great armed chair, unless the chairs are all so. If you meet the person you are to visit in the open air, don't put on your hat, till he puts on his, or till he begs you to be covered. *Principles of Politeness.*

If a superior accompanies you to his house, and makes a sign for you to enter first, or to get into his carriage, do it instantly, never dispute it with him, or hang back through respect; for here respect is, to submit to his decision: be assured he knows his rank, (it is what every man studies) and does not want to be reminded of it: so, if he stands speaking to you with his hat in his hand, or rises from his seat to receive you, it would be ill breeding to say, "I beg my Lord, or I beg Sir you will be covered—or keep your seat." It might pass very well from him to you, but not from you to him.*

*If he desires you to sit, sit; if he offers you the upper hand, take it; if he urges you to approach, do it; to be too ceremonious is to be impertinent; if in the course of conversation, he rises to speak to you, you should rise also.

From a superior to an inferior, familiarity is not only tolerable, but obliging; but from an inferior to a superior, especially where there is no degree of intimacy, it is not only unbecoming, but insolent.— *Principles of Politeness.*

If you are offered precedence by superiors, take it; it is uncivil to refuse it. An English Nobleman being in France, was told by Louis XIV, to enter his coach before him, he hung back with a false modesty; the king immediately got in, ordering the door to be shut, drove on, leaving the nobleman behind.

If in your visits to this superior, you find him engaged in conversation with another; after the first salute, it will be unmannerly by addressing him, either to draw him from the conversation he is engaged in, or to attempt to take off his attention from the subject he is upon; you are either to wait till he speaks to you, or to address some other person, if present, not engaged, and more upon an equality.*

    *If a man of rank, a superior, makes you a visit, and you know of his coming, it is a mark of respect to meet him at his coach door, and having brought him into the best room of the house, reach him a chair, and when he begs you to sit, seat yourself by him, one in a chair without arms.

    If he surprises you busy in your chamber, quit all employment while he stays, unless he enjoins you to the contrary. It is a duty indeed we owe to every visitant, whether superior or equal, to treat them with marked respect.

    When a person of rank makes you a visit, it is not respectful to suffer him to wait long, unless you are engaged with persons of greater rank, in which case, 'tis right, if you can, to send a person of condition, to entertain him, till you come.

    When your visitant leaves you, wait on him to his coach; if it be a lady, offer her your hand, but with a glove on, and having helped her into her carriage, wait at the coach door uncovered, till her carriage is gone.

    If there be many persons with you and one of them goes away, the rest staying behind, if he that goes away, be of more rank than the rest, you should leave them, and wait on him out; if of less, you should let him go alone, only making an excuse; if their condition be equal, regulate your conduct by your intimacy.

    If whist you are speaking to a nobleman, another should enter the room, but of inferior rank, you are not to drop your conversation with the first, or introduce an inferior by name, but bowing only to the second comer, continue talking as before. Should the person you are talking to, break off, and address the new comer, you may do the same; it is improper at any time to introduce an inferior to a superior, unless at the superior's request.

    In short, to point out all the particulars of your conduct, in order to be respectful, would be tedious to the last degree, it is best learned by imitation. A young man should take notice how well-bred people act, in company with their superiors, and endeavour, as far as possible, to follow their example.—*Principles of Politeness*.

There is a decent familiarity necessary in the course of life; mere formal visits, upon formal invitations, are not the thing; this creates no connexion, nor will they prove of service to you: it is careless and easy ingress and egress, at all hours, that secures an acquaintance to our interest, and this is acquired by a respectful familiarity entered into, without forfeiting your consequence.—*Principles of Politeness*.

If you receive letters of introduction to any one residing in a place to which you are going, this letter should be delivered to you personally, as soon after you arrive as possible; to let any length of time slip between the date of the letter, and the time of delivering it, unless your excuse be an exceeding good one, is disrespectful, if it cannot be avoided, the best apology that can be made, *should* be made.

With Respect To Equals

The above measures are not so immediately necessary; you may fall in, as you find it convenient, without this restraint, and act as your good sense and good manners shall direct you:* but

*When an expected guest comes to dine with you, if your equal, or indeed not greatly your inferior, he should be sure to find your family in order, and yourself dressed, and ready to receive him with a smiling countenance. This inspires an immediate cheerfulness into your guest, and persuades him of your esteem, and desire of his company; you are not to suffer him to knock a considerable time before he gains admittance, and then the door being opened by a maid, or some improper servant, who wonders where the devil all the men are, and being asked if her master is at home, answers, "She believes he is," and conducts you into a hall or back-parlour, where you stay some time before you, in *dishabiles*, wait on him, from your study, or your garden, ask pardon, and assure your friend that you did not suspect him so soon!—*Fielding on Conversation.*

When your guest offers to go, if it be in the country, there should be no solicitation to stay, unless for the whole night, and that so farther than to give him a moral assurance of his being welcome so to do. No assertions that he shan't go yet, no laying on violent hands, no private orders to servants to delay preparing the horses or vehicle, and entitle your friend to an action of false imprisonment!—*Fielding on Conversation.*

With Respect To Inferiors

You will, I dare say, feel yourself disposed to shew all that good nature, and condescension that will tend to make you beloved. If you at any time stoop to associate with such, your plan is to study to conduct yourself so, that they shall not feel their inferiority. On this head, I am persuaded that I need say no more. I have said a good deal respecting it in *The Principles of Politeness*, as I have with regard to polite attention both to women and men, in company or elsewhere.—All there is wanting in

Conversation

is as follows:

The young man in company with his superiors, such as I have above pointed out, must not be loud, boisterous, dogmatical, or dictatorial, but modest, diffident, and unassuming; not giving the lead in conversation, but taking it up as he finds it; not speaking till another has done, but even stopping short, if a man of more intelligence, experience, and knowledge of the subject, shall presume to interrupt him; I say, *presume*, for it will sometimes happen that men of years and science, will claim the privilege of being heard in preference to the young and unexperienced, in despite of the usual forms of punctilio and good manners; in such case, a modest giving way is sure to conciliate esteem. Besides, we often gain more knowledge by conversation, than by study. Solomon, the wisest of men, says, "As iron sharpeneth iron, so doth the face of a man his friend."

If we are talking to men of science, it is better to be silent, than expose our own ignorance; but if the subject be such as we are acquainted with, a modest reply from the youngest man in company, to the most aged, cannot give offence; it might be introduced with "I beg pardon Sir, in differing from you, but it strikes me so and so; if I am wrong, I will thank you to set me right." In such case, any absurdity a young man may broach, or any futile argument he may advance, will be good naturedly overlooked and considered.*

*To intrude upon or interrupt the discourse, when a superior is speaking to another, is want of respect; so it is to correct or assist his memory this being little else than an indirect way of giving him the lie.— *Principles of Politeness.*

Whilst I am thus recommending modesty and diffidence, be assured I must condemn any ill-natured sneer or contemptuous derision, even of those we may conceive below us in understanding. Such conduct not only argues folly, but rudeness, and may give rise to contention, which of all things in conversation should be avoided, and if persisted in, might lead to dispute and quarrelling.*

*Never be witty at the expence of any one present, nor gratify that idle inclination too strong in most young men, I mean laughing at, or ridiculing the weakness or infirmities of others, by way of diverting the company; it may gain the laugh on your side, for the present, but it will make the person at whose expence you are merry, your enemy for ever after. You may shine, but take care not to scorch; no intimacy or friendship, gives a privilege to say things that shock; a joke if it carries a sting with it, is no longer a joke, but an affront.—*Principles of Politeness.*

If the young man posses a brilliancy of parts, he may shew it off, so that he does not wound, or reflect upon any one of the company, or their absent friends. Some men are so hardy as not to lose a jest or a bon mot,[7] even at the sacrifice of a friend: whoever indulges himself in this way may *lose* a friend, but is not in the way to *gain* one. Pleasantries may enliven conversation, and are allowable, but not at the expence of truth or honour, or the respect due to those with whom we associate.

Choice Of Acquaintance.

I have in the book I have so often alluded to, said much on this head, but will drop a word or two more on the occasion here.

If a young gentleman herds with low bred men, and men of abandoned character, it is as natural to suppose that he will catch some low-bred maxims, and customs, as that he would be infected with their contagious distemper, if he was to visit them when sick. The pride and folly of some men are such, that they covet to be thought the king of their company, and on this principle are too often seen reveling with their inferiors: the old adage, "tell me what company you keep, and I will tell you what you are," is a just one, and it is verified by experience, that he who wishes to be the best man in the company he keeps will soon become the worst of any company he comes into; for he that makes himself an ass, invites others to ride him; Seneca used to say, that he never went among low or disorderly men, but he came home a worse man than when he went out. You may chance to meet with in life a person or two of this cast, even among the gentry, but it will be but one or two, for gentlemen in general, if they find a man so disposed, will, if

---

[7] French term for a witty remark.

already admitted among them, soon desert him; is not admitted, will be cautious how they receive him. Be assured, the best mode of being respected as a gentleman is, to associate with such and such only.*

*Every person who indulges his ill nature or vanity at the expence of others, high titled as he may be, is thoroughly ill bred.— *Fielding on Conversation.*

Depend upon it, in the estimation of mankind, you will sink or rise to the level of the company you keep.—*Principles of Politeness.*

Sensible of the necessity of this, a Derbyshire Baronet, who unexpectedly came into possession of the title and a fortune sufficient to support it, took the following step to obtain respect of the neighbouring gentry.

He was a man of no education, and lived by writing for attornies, and thus earned about a guinea[8] a week; his wife was the daughter of a bricklayer, a decent woman, who, to add to their income, took in linen to clear-starch. He was respected among his equals, and his usual rendezvous in the evening was an alehouse. On coming to this title and fortune, after he was settled in the family mansion, he made an entertainment and invited all his old acquaintance with their wives; treated them hospitably and kindly, after dinner addressed them in the following manner, "Gentlemen, it has pleased Providence, to bless me with distinction and an ample fortune, to raise me from the obscure situation I have been long in, and place me in a more exalted one: though pride is no part of my composition, I know too well what is due to that situation of life, I am now to move in, and the class of people I shall be expected to associate with; prudence will oblige me therefore to drop all my old acquaintance; but, in dropping them, I shall never lose sight of their friendships to me, nor the happiness I have enjoyed in their

---

[8] Approximately £1.1.0.

society. I trust you all wish me so well as not to be displeased at this resolution; for was I to keep company with you, as I have hitherto done, I should not be received into that which my fortune entitles me to expect, and then I should disgrace my ancestry; this I never mean to do. I shall from this time always be happy to hear of your well doing, and if at any time it should be in my power to be of any use to you, I shall cheerfully do it; but you must in good nature excuse my associating with you as before, and not think the worse of me for this candid declaration." His company took it in good part, wished him joy, health and happiness, and promised that, if they could not increase it, they would never interrupt it.

This sensible conduct soon got wind among the gentlemen of the county: they approved it, and not long after, he made a second entertainment, invited them and their ladies; his house was filled, and his former situation was forgotten.

Whatever you do then, young man, select your friends from among the virtuous of your own class; be as kind as you please to those below you, but never suffer them to exclude you from the society of *gentlemen*.

This not being a moral treatise, I shall not enter into the necessity of recommending to you not to mix or live with the abandoned, even of your own class. If you respect yourself, or wish to be respected, you will never be seen in company with those dissipated men of fashion, who spend their hours either at a tavern, a gaming-house, or a brothel.*

*Be it then your ambition to get into the best company, and when there, emulate their virtues, but not their vices. You have no doubt, often heard of genteel and fashionable vices; these are, whoring, drinking, and gaming. It has happened, that some men, even with these vices, have been admired and esteemed; understand this rightly; it is not their vices for which they are admired, but for some accomplishments they at the same time possess; for their parts, their learning, or their good-breeding:

be assured, were they free from these vices, they would be much more esteemed. In these mixed characters, the bad part is overlooked, for the sake of the good.—*Principles of Politeness*.

Keeping Acquaintance

Having selected your acquaintance, the next art is to keep it. This is done by attention and cultivation. "He who hath friends, must shew himself friendly," so says the Wisest of men, at a very early age, and 'tis even the same at the present day. The pride of man's heart is such, that if they think their acquaintance slighted, they will slight you in return. Chance or introduction brings men acquainted, but this acquaintance must be cherished and cultivated, or it will end as readily as it began.

To keep up acquaintance it is requisite to be in the habit of inviting and interchanging civilities; the greater the intercourse between friends, the more they become and the more we are at ease with them. One respectable friend introduces us to the knowledge and acquaintance of another, and by reciprocal respect and attention, such acquaintance improves into friendship.

If a superior condescends to pay you the first morning visit, as it will sometimes happen, from your residing in his neighbourhood, and wishing to be acquainted with you; return that visit as soon as possible, within a day or two. This will be proof of the honour you conceive done you: if it be an equal that pays you the first visit, you may return it at the first convenient opportunity, but never delay it longer than about a fortnight, lest it should be concluded as want of respect. If the first visit is to any neighbour, by *you*, and he should not be at home, never fail to leave a card, with your name on it, and place of abode; lest he should not be made acquainted with the visit you made him. If he receives your card, and does not return your visit, he means not to cultivate your acquaintance; if you have any doubt, whether your card was delivered, you may either pay him a second visit or not, as you think proper.

The first visit paid, and returned, they may be interchanged once in three or four weeks, or oftener, if you wish to be intimate; but intimacy seldom takes place, unless the parties meet still more frequent, either at their own houses, or at the house of some common friend; it is eating and drinking together, and uniting in parties, that create intimacy and friendship; otherwise, a man may visit for years, and scarce personally know the person visited; such things have happened, for as leaving your name on a card at the door, is considered as a visit, this may go on reciprocally for a length of time, and if such visitors never meet at home, they do not personally know each other, when they chance to meet at any common friend's house, or elsewhere; and of course such meeting would be very awkward.

On paying visits of ceremony, care should be taken not to make them too long, nor too frequent; a quarter of an hour, or twenty minutes, is sufficient time to exchange compliments, or run over the topics of the day; but if the visitors become congenial to each other, and intimacy succeeds, times and lengths of visits, need not be pointed out, they will direct themselves.

Visits of ceremony in the country, are not expected, if beyond the reach of a morning's ride.

Cards

Have been introduced, lest the carelessness or stupidity of servants, or their multiplicity of messages should lead them into mistakes, and occasion disappointments and errors—but they cannot be too short or concise, provided they are explicit.

The following is a proper card of invitation to dinner, if to a superior; but this card should be enclosed in a cover, and sealed, and properly directed;

1. "Mr. R— requests the honour of Lord B—'s company on Wednesday next to dinner at five."

Grosvenor-street, Feb. 5.

Or if in a letter,

2. "Do me the honour my dear Lord, to take your dinner (or your soup) with me on Wednesday next at five and you will meet Lord S—, Sir Thomas L—, and some of your acquaintance."

From your Lordship's

Respectful Servant,

Grosvenor-street, Feb. 5. J. R—.

Answered.

3. My dear Sir,

"Were I disengaged on Wednesday next, I would join your party with pleasure, and am sincerely yours,"

Manchester-square, Feb. 5.

B—.

Or in answer to the Card, No. 1.

> 4. "Lord B—'s compliments to Mr. R—, and will do himself the pleasure of waiting on him!"

Manchester-square, Feb. 5.

If the invitation be to an equal, the word *favor* may be substituted for *honor*, as in No. 1.

If to an Inferior, the card should convey *compliments*, as in No. 4.

On receiving an invitation in writing, never omit to return an answer in writing, and that as soon as possible. Though *compliments* from a superior are passed in a card to you; I conceive it more respectful to omit that term in your reply (unless you use *respects* or *best compliments*, as implying something more humble) and word your answer thus:

> 5. Mr. R—, will do himself the honour of waiting on Lord B—, at the hour appointed.

Grosvenor-street, Feb. 7.

If you are going home for any length of time, a visit of ceremony is necessary, in order to take leave. If the party be not at home, leave a card with your name only, writing under it,—*To take leave.*

Superscription To Letters, Cards, &C.

To a Baron…The Rt. Hon. Lord B—

To a Baroness…The Rt. Hon. Lady B—

To a Viscount…Viscount C—

To a Viscountess…Viscountess C—

To an Earl…Earl D—

To a Countess…Countess D—

To a Marquis…Marquis of E—

To a Marchioness…Marchioness of E—

To a Duke…The Duke of F—

To a Duchess…The Duchess of F—

To an Archbishop…The Lord Archbp. of

To a Bishop…The Lord Bishop of

*Bishops' Ladies are only stiled [styled] Mrs. with the name of the Bishop.

To a Dean…The Revd. Dean of

To a Doctor…Revd. John D—

Not a Doctor…Revd. John D—

Not the Revd.…Mr. John E—

To a Lord's son not titled, the Hon. J. D—, without Esq.

To a Gentleman, John E—, Esq. if a Member of Parliament, add M. P. Without this addition, his letters by the post do not pass free.

Never send letters to a Peer, or a Member of Parliament, by the two-penny post, in London, as they do not pass free by such conveyance; many persons of rank, have forbid the receipt of such letters at their houses, that they may not be troubled with trifling applications. If in cities and towns, and within small distances; it is a proper mark of respect, to send such letters by a servant, or some private hand.

To an Ambassador…To his Excellency.

Esquire is an arbitrary title, flattering to most men, and is generally made use of in directing to gentlemen who live on their means, merchants, aldermen, barristers, and men of large property, even if in trade.

When addressing noblemen in conversation, if under the rank of a duke, we always say, *My Lord*, and *Your Lordship*, but this last only occasionally, if used too often, it is fulsome. If you speak to a duke, we say, *My Lord Duke*, and *Your Grace*; if to a prince, *Sir*, and *Your Royal Highness*. If other noblemen are present, and you wish to address one in particular, under the rank of a duke, you address him thus, *Lord Exeter*, tho' a marquis; *Lord Ligonier*, tho' an earl; but if a duke, we say, if there is but one present, *Duke*, or *My Lord Duke*; if more than one, *Duke of Richmond*, *Duke of Athol*, and so on; but never abbreviate their titles, as calling on *Lord Ex*. or another *Lord Lig*. This would be rude, because too familiar, unless you are of superior or equal rank, and even then it would be ungenteel.

To ladies of quality, we never say, *My Lady*; their servants, so address them, but not their acquaintance; but *yes*, *Madam*, and *no*, *Madam*, using *your Ladyship* occasionally, as we do *your Lordship*, when speaking to a nobleman.

So when we write to any Lord, under the rank of Duke, we begin with *My Lord*, if to a Duke, *My Lord Duke*; if to a woman of quality, *Madam*, even to a Duchess, and never use the expression, *Lordship*, *Ladyship*, or *Grace*, but once or twice in a letter, and that principally, where you may have occasion to allude to their rank, their power, or their influence, as for example:

6.   "My Lord,

I have taken the liberty to write to your *Lordship*, to say that the horse *you* bought of T. B. is by no means a sound one. It is an imposition on your Lordship, and if the man had served me so, I would return him, &c."

But with a little study, letters to noblemen, may be so penned, as not to have occasion to introduce the words, *you* or *yours* in any part of it, of course *Lordship* need not be substituted for either. The above might have been worded thus:

7.   "My Lord,

Indulge me with the liberty of saying, that the horse which T. B. sold to your Lordship, is by no means sound, and had he so imposed upon me, I would have returned it, &c."

If you are in intimacy with a nobleman, or his lady, your letters may begin with *My dear Lord*, or, *Dear Madam*, and may end in a similar way, as,

8.   I have the honor to be *my Lord*, or *my dear Lord*, *Madam*, or *my dear Madam*, —*your Lordship's*, or *your Ladyship's* most respectful servant, —or I remain with all due respect, *your Lordship's*, as me be.

Such are the *usual* forms, but they may be varied at the writer's discretion: all that is necessary is, that when writing to superiors, we should express ourselves with becoming humility, and deference, and not omit giving them to understand, that we have not lost sight of their rank: when writing to friends, we are to be respectful and friendly.

Archbishops are addressed thus, *my Lord*, or *your Grace*.

Bishops, *my Lord*, or *your Lordship*.

Their sons and daughters, as plain gentlemen, *Madam*, or *Mrs.*

To Deans, we usually say, *Mr. Dean;* to Military Men, we give in conversation or writing, (if above a Captain in the army, or a Lieutenant in the navy, who ranks as a Captain in the army,) their military titles, as *General* A——, *Colonel* B——, *Major* C——, *Admiral* D——, *Commodore* E——, *Captain* F——.

In our epistles to superiors, if we wish to be thought respectful, the paper on which we write, should be good, and not less than a sheet, the ink black, and the handwriting intelligible, and without any abbreviations; and this sheet whether sent through the post-office or not, or whether the person you write to, be a member of either house of parliament or not, of course though the expence of postage be double, it is not regarded, if the person you write to be opulent; I say in any of these cases, the sheet you write on, should be enclosed in an *envelope* or cover, provided, if sent by the post, the enclosed and its cover, does not exceed in weight one ounce, so as to prevent its passing free to a Peer or Member of Parliament, or double postage to any other friend; for to suppose your friend (unless he had a small circumscribed fortune) will grudge double postage, is to suppose him penurious and mean. On the same principle, never think of freeing a post letter, by paying the postage, unless it be to one to whom you are convinced the expence of postage will be inconvenient or disagreeable.

Precedency, &C.

When invited to dinner, make a point of always being there in proper time, not to make the company wait; fifteen minutes at least before the appointed hour, and to prevent mistakes, see that your watch goes right, and make a proper allowance for the time in going. A superior indeed, will not wait your coming beyond the time; and if you enter after the company is seated, you are a general disturber.

In paying dinner visits, and where you expect to meet company, your dress should be better than ordinary, by no means in boots; in receiving visits at home, dress is not so necessary.

On your entering the room where the company is, address yourself first to the lady of the house, next to the master, and after, to the rest of the company you are introduced to, by a respectful bow to each. No saluting of ladies now, by kissing them, as was the custom some years back. If you are acquainted with any of the company, after your compliments are paid to the mistress and master of the house, to bow and address the rest, according to their rank, is proper; to the ladies first, and then the gentlemen.

It is necessary, prior to dinner, to look round, and consider the several degrees of rank of the company present, and there may be no confusion in walking into the room where the table is served. The table of precedency at the end of this volume, will help you out. The ladies of course will go first; and without the trouble of marshalling them, every woman of fashion knows her own rank and will walk out first, second, or third, according to that rank. Suppose a Duchess, a Countess, and a Viscountess, be present, the Duchess will take the lead, the Countess will follow, and the Viscountess next, let their ages be what they may. In no woman of quality is present, the eldest married woman takes the lead, then the eldest unmarried woman, and so on.

Gentlemen proceed in the same order; but where the master of the house directs. Seats are table, are taken generally in the like manner, the ladies at the upper end of the table, the gentlemen at the lower; but the master or mistress of the house will sometimes direct it otherwise, and seat the ladies and gentlemen alternately, that is one gentleman and one lady, and so on, for convenience.

When the men and women are so mixed, it is a mark of good manners to carve and help the ladies, to any dish that may be near you.*

* Use with a little attention, is all that is requisite to acquit yourself well in this particular.—*Principles of Politeness*. The art of carving may soon be acquired, by means of a little book I have published, with wooden cuts, called *The Honours of the Table*.—Prince 4s.

Wiping a plate with your napkin is rude, the whole service of the table among the opulent is naturally clean; if a plate accidently be otherwise, call to a servant for another.

Drinking of health during dinner or supper, among the first class of people is entirely exploded; but if the master of the house sets the example, you may follow it.

Call for any wine you please, without waiting to be asked; in some houses, the master announce to his company, the different sorts of wine on the side-board; in great houses, where this is not done, all common wines are supposed to be present. At the house of a friend, you are expected to be as much at your ease, as if at home, and of course may freely ask for any wine, you know the master is accustomed to keep, whether it is on the side-board or not, and whether before dinner or after. But this liberty is seldom taken by those, who do not give the same liberty at their own houses.

But I cannot do better than to recommend a young person to read a little tract I have published, called *The Honors of the Table*, now in its third edition, wherein he will see the conduct he should observe, whether visitor or visited; this will teach him at some time, the whole art of carving, illustrated by cuts, how to acquit himself with gracefulness and respect to his company.

"To do the honors of a table gracefully, is one of the outlines of a well-bred man, and to carve well, little as it may seem, is useful twice every day, and the doing of which ill, is not only troublesome to ourselves, but renders is disagreeable and ridiculous to others."—*Lord Chesterfield's Letters*.

When you wish to depart before the rest of the company, never take out your watch to see the hour, as this would seem to remind others of the time; nor take any leave, but what they call a French leave, and which our polite neighbours, the French, have instructed us in, that is to steal off as unnoticed as possible, for if you chuse to go, it is necessary that you drag others with you.*

*French leave was introduced, that on one person leaving the company, the rest might not be disturbed; looking at your watch, does what that piece of politeness was designed to prevent; it is a kind dictating to all present, and telling them it is time, or almost time to break up.—*Principles of Politeness*.

Vails to servants are never given; of course, to offer a servant a piece of money, is an affront to the master; it is as much as to say, that he cannot afford to pay his own attendants.

If cards are introduced, it is not necessary to play, if you dislike it, unless indeed there are not sufficient persons to make up a party without you; but even in that case, you may be excused, if you are never known to play elsewhere; at no rate attempt to play at whist, or quadrille, if you do not play tolerably, for if you should be indifferent about losing your own money, you ought not to be so with respect to that of others, and though your partner may say little, he will think the more. If you *do* sit down to play, never wrangle, or find the least fault with your partner's play; it will not mend him, of course it will do no good, and always give great offence.*

*If desired to play at cards, deeper than you would, refuse it ludicrously; tell them if you were sure to lose you might possible sit down, but, that as fortune may be favorable, you dread the thought of having too much money, ever since you found, what an incumbrance it was to poor Harlequin, and therefore you are determined not to put yourself in a way of winning, more than such and such a sum a day. This light way of declining invitations to vice and folly, is better than a sententious refusal, which would be laughed at: never receive your winnings with elation, or lose your temper with your money.—*Principles of Politeness*.

If invited to drink at any man's house, more than you think is wholesome, you may say, "you wish you could, but so little makes you both drunk and sick, that you should only be bad company by doing it, of course beg to be excused."—*Principles of Politeness*.

There can be no greater instance of a weak and pusillanimous temper, than for a man to pass his whole life in opposition to his own understanding, and not dare to be, what he thinks be ought to be, or to betray a fear of not appearing singular. Singularity is always laudable, when it adheres to the dictates of honor, conscience, and morality, and is only censurable when it makes men act contrary to reason. For example, it is bad in a modest young gentleman, who has not the confidence to refuse his glass, till he grows so elated and flushed with wine, as to engross all the talk to himself, or abuse every one present; it is bad in any young man, that is afraid to refuse an invitation to a tavern, to drink to excess, or go to any improper place, or to commit any other extravagance proposed; and this under a fear of being thought covetous, to have no money, or to be under the controul of his parents, or friends; when in fact his pride should be in the free exercise of his understanding, and in daring to speak his free sentiments.—*Principles of Politeness*.

A dignity of character is best acquired by a certain firmness in all our actions; a mean, timid, and passive compliance, lets a man down more than he is aware of.—*Principles of Politeness*.

As to rules of conversation, which are as necessary as the common modes of attention and respect, if we expect to be esteemed; I must refer you to the *Principles of Politeness*, where I have said a great deal on this subject, and pointed them out in almost every possible case; as also on cleanliness of person and dress; for an inattention to this, is a marked rudeness to the company you mix with.

Gallantry

This is a subject I shall but tenderly touch on, knowing, that if I am either too rigid, or too strict in my precepts, I shall be little attended to. It is a matter that should be rather be left to the discretion and feelings of those who have received a good and a virtuous education, as I suppose those of whom I here write to have had: but I hope and trust, that a word or two may be thrown in, without giving offence.

If gallantry to the ladies, be considered as part of the accomplishments of a gentleman, it is that only which consists in a respectful and lively attention, perhaps addressed to their vanity, their beauty, or their good sense. If you do not make yourself agreeable to the women, you will assuredly lose ground among the men; but as a man of sense, I would never compliment a lady at the expence of the truth.

But what I most aim at under this head, is, to advise you to steer clear of giving any particular lady to understand, that you are more attached to her than others; unless the case be really so, and you mean to pursue it up with honor. Such misrepresentations on your part, and misconceptions on hers, may lead to entanglements, attended with ruinous consequences. Let your attention to the women be general, and general only; and if you find among your female acquaintance, one more partial and attentive to you than ordinary, after consulting your own heart, and perhaps advising with your best friends, if you discover that a matrimonial alliance with that lady, would be imprudent, and not what you like; withdraw your attention immediately, and not suffer any attachment either on her side or yours, to take place. It is better to avoid meeting such lady in future, than by throwing yourself in her way, increase a flame perhaps already kindled, that may tend both to her unhappiness and yours and draw you into a scrape with some of her male relations. Such conduct would be unworthy the character of a gentleman, and a man of humanity.

If this first step is condemnable, to carry it further to the ruin of an unfortunate female, whose only error in life, may be thinking too favorably of you, would be barbarity, and every thing this is unmanly, and low.

There is no being a real gentleman, without honor, and a becoming pride, and surely there is no becoming pride in seduction, for the seducer in any shape is a rascal, and lost to every sense of virtue, and of honor.

Should this hapless female be a gentlewoman, her brother may call you to account. Should she be a wife, both the law and her husband may combine to punish you, and ruin you, and let her be what she will, the rational part of mankind will despise you, and Heaven will revenge her cause.

Dueling

What shall I say of this horrid practice? The most favourable construction I can put upon this crime, is, that like the murder of a bastard child, by its ill-fated mother, is arises from a sense of shame and honor in the perpetrator; but still 'tis murder; for no *good* end can justify a *bad* act. "We are not to do evil, that good may come (says St. Paul,) whose damnation is just."

The duelist who puts his antagonist to death, to support his honor; and thro' fear of being branded with cowardice, is no less criminal than the woman who puts her child to death, to preserve her honor, and conceal her shame. Both are guilty of murder, and though the law punishes the latter with death, and winks at the former, in compliance with prejudice, reconciling it under the idea of self-defence; yet God, who sees not as a man seeth, will punish both one and the other.

What is this sense of shame which the duelist dreads?—The contempt of a set of miscreants brought up in horrid notions, which good men as much despise, as they do the opinions and conduct of the bravo who makes murder a profession.

A man may almost as well reason with a madman, as one of this stamp; at least at the time when his choler is up, and reflection has left him; but in hopes of doing away such pernicious prejudices, and saving a life or two, at some future time, I will venture to reason with my young readers, in the cool moments of consideration, when he does me the honor of taking up my book, and giving this part a reading.

I will first shew him the *absurdity* of the practice, and next point out the mode of avoiding a recourse to it; without either loss of honor or fear of being called a coward, by men of sense and virtue; as to the opinions of other men, they are not worth regarding; a man may as well be called a *coward* as a *fool*.

To say that a brave man does not fear death, is idle; in a *good* cause, he will naturally risk his life; but is a *bad* one, he has every reason to dread it. Life is a man's last stake, and let our expectations be whatever they may be, hereafter,

—we naturally fear

To be, I know not what— I know not where.

Life is desirable to all men, and he that declares the contrary, is a fool, and will not be believed.

This fear which drives men to risk their lives in duels, does not, I am persuaded, arise from a wish to make their friends suppose that they dare to die; but from a dread of being excluded from their society. This exclusion proceeds from mistaken notions; I will endeavour to remove them.

Dueling is called *demanding*, and *giving satisfaction;* and it is the etiquette generally on these occasions, that the challenger or party aggrieved, has the choice of weapons, and if pistols are determined on, to have the first fire; and the party challenged, being the aggressor, is to stand quietly to be shot at, when, if he is not killed or rendered unable to return the fire, it is at his option either to fire at his antagonist, or discharge his pistol in the air; if he does the latter, the affair ends, and the challenger has had the christian *satisfaction* of trying to *murder* his enemy, whom his Redeemer directs him to *love*.

But where is the *satisfaction* the challenger receives in standing a contest *life for life*, with the person who has barely *affronted* him? If he deems the affronter to be a scoundrel; why give this scoundrel a chance of taking away his life?

What *satisfaction* can arise, or what gratification can there be, in giving a man whom we detest, an opportunity of hurrying us out of the world, or maiming us for the remainder of our life?

Recollect that a man so hurried to the bar of Judgement, without repentance, if there be any truth in christianity, is irrevocably lost; for though he may have made his peace with Heaven, the hour before; his aiming at the life of his adversary; and falling in the conflict, being the last act of his life, admits of no repentance; and he dies as much a murderer, as if he had killed his antagonist, and survived his fall: for our Saviour says, "He that hateth his brother, and would destroy him if he could, is a *murderer*; and no murderer can inherit the Kingdom of Heaven."— Poor *satisfaction* this—it is taking revenge upon himself!

Admitting that he kills his antagonist,—What then?—What *satisfaction* can arise from a tormenting conscience, for having robbed perhaps a parent of his child, a child of its parent, or a wife of her husband; and having sent a poor wretch out of his life, perhaps very unprepared to go? The late Lord Pomfret,[9] who challenged and killed Mr. Gray,[10] in a duel, uniformly declared, thro' his life, that he never enjoyed a peaceful moment after.

---

[9] George Fermor, 2nd Earl of Pomfret (1722-1785).

[10] "His Lordship, when Lord Lempster, had the misfortune to be compelled to fight a duel with Captain Grey, who fell in the combat: He was tried, and found guilty of man-slaughter," from "*A* Compendious PEERAGE *of* ENGLAND, *continued from Page* 321 *of our* MAGAZINE *for* December *last*; *containing a* GENEALOGICAL ACCOUNT *of the Noble Family of* FERMOR, Earl of POMFRET, *with their* ARMS *accurately engraved*," in *The Universal Magazine of Knowledge and Pleasure*, February 1777, pg. 98.

But cries the challenger—Revenge is sweet.—But not at the risk of one's own life? This is revenging it on *himself*. How would this revenger feel, should his antagonist have so far the advantage as to disarm him, and make him beg his life? Where is the *satisfaction* in such a case?—What mortification must it be to a proud spirited man to beg for mercy, and even for his very existence, to him, whom ten minutes before, he esteemed a villain, and his greatest enemy?—What consolation can honor afford for such disgrace?

The *absurdity* of this practice must then be very evident.— Let us next consider how it may be avoided without loss of honor, or the imputation of cowardice.—The best mode and the surest, to remove an *effect*, is to take away the *cause*. Give no cause of offence then, and never mix with quarrelsome men.

There are some men that will quarrel for straws. A prudent man will fly such company, as he would a ruinous house in a storm; lest a brick or a tile should fall upon head and kill him.

Lord Chesterfield says, "Remember there are but two alternatives for a gentleman; politeness, or the sword." Be civil then, even to those you detest, and not notice affronts, unless they are very glaring. But should you at any time be so affronted in public company, as not be able to pass it over; be cool, make no reply, retire, and before you determine to resent it, seek out some dispassionate man of sense and experience, (not an officer, for their notions of honor, are in a great measure regulated by what is professional) and consult him on the occasion; state the matter coolly and truly to him, and ask him in what manner it is to be got over, without disgracing yourself, or proceeding to extremities, and be governed by his advice. He will most possibly undertake to adjust it amicably.*

*Politeness to those we do not respect is no more a breach of faith, than your *humble Servants*, at the bottom of a challenge; they are universally understood to be things of course.—*Principles of Politeness*.

If fools should be at any time, attempt to be witty upon you, the best way is, not to know their witticisms are levelled at you, and to conceal any uneasiness it may give you; but should they be so plain, that you cannot be thought ignorant of their meanings, I would recommend, rather than quarrel with the company, joining even in the laugh against yourself; allow the jest to be a good one, and take it in seeming good humour.—Never attempt to retaliate the same way, as that would imply you were hurt. Should what is said wound your honor, or your moral character, there is but one proper alternative, which I hope you will never have recourse to.—*Principles of Politeness*.

Wrangling and quarrelling are characteristics of a weak mind.—*Ditto*.

A man who cannot hear displeasing things without visible marks of anger or uneasiness, is at the mercy of every knave. You may tell me that coolness must be natural, if not, you can never acquire it. I will admit the force of constitution; but people are very apt to blame that for many things they might readily avoid. Care, with a little reflection, will soon give you the mastery of your temper. If you find yourself the subject to sudden starts of passion, determine with yourself, not to utter a single word till your reason has recovered itself, and resolve to keep your countenances as unmoved as possible.

In the course of life, we shall find it necessary very often, to bear with very ill tempers, as we do with copper money, for the benefit of commerce; and to put on a pleasing countenance, when we are exceedingly displeased: we must frequently seem friendly, when we are quite otherwise. I am sensible it is difficult to accost a man with smiles, whom we know to be our enemy:—but what is to be done? On receiving an affront, if you cannot be justified in knocking the offender down, you must not notice the offence; for in the eyes of the world, taking an offence calmly, is considered as cowardice.—*Principles of Politeness*.

If you are in the army, or navy, refer the matter to your commanding officer. If he can settle it, he will. Military men are rather in an awkward predicament. The articles of war acquit a man of cowardice in refusing a challenge, and break him if he accepts it; but on the other hand, if he does not accept it, his brother officers will send him to Coventry[11], that is, not associate with, nor associate with, nor speak to him, except on duty, and he will thus obliged to quit the regiment.

An officer is punishable by a court martial, if he challenges his commanding officer, and such commanding officer will proceed against him legally, thus taking advantage of his situation; the idea of cowardice never occurs to him, nor urges him to fight, if he can with propriety avoid it; a proof that nothing spurs him to risk his life, in order to revenge an insult, but fear of being sent to Coventry. The Duke of York[12] waved this distinction, and fought with Col. Lenox,[13] who challenged him.

Offence is often given by speaking disrespectfully of another; this was what Col. Lenox charged the Duke of York, his commanding officer, with doing. Be careful then, never to fall into this womanish, silly habit, of entertaining one friend at the expence of another; it may come round when it is not expected. Such conduct is often the cause of quarrels.*

*Never tell in one company, what you see or hear in another. Things apparently indifferent, may, when often repeated, and told abroad, have much more serious consequences than imagined. In conversation there is a tacit reliance, that what is said, will not be repeated, and a man, though not enjoined to secrecy, will be excluded company, if found to be

---

[11] English idiom meaning to deliberately ostracize someone. The person being targeted is treated as if they were invisible and inaudible.

[12] Prince Frederick, Duke of York and Albany (1763-1827).

[13] Charles Lennox, 4th Duke of Richmond (1764-1819). The duel occurred in 1789, stemming for an allegation made by the Duke of York that Colonel Lennox failed to respond to an insult like a gentleman.

a tattler; besides he will draw himself into a thousand scrapes, and every one will be afraid to speak before him.—*Principles of Politeness*.

I am happy to find that gentlemen, men of honor, and even military men in some cases, appeal to the civil laws of their country, when challenged, instead of the sword; and they appear to be countenanced in so doing.

I conceive no man to be a coward that has sufficient spirit to defend himself against an assailant; and it is time enough for a man to draw his sword, when he is attacked. He should learn the use of this weapon, and be perfect master of it, (for pistols are never produced at a rencontre,) but he should never use it except in self-defense.

Let no man suppose that not resisting a robber on the highway, is a mark of cowardice; what man in his senses would stand a pistol shot for a few guineas, or risk his life in a cause where his honor is not at stake? I have the authority of Field Marshal, John, Earl of Ligonier, Commander in Chief,[14] on this head. His courage, his honor, his magnanimity, were undisputed, and yet he declared to me, that he would never stand a contest with a robber, lose what he might.

There is another consideration that I think should deter a man from dueling, this is the necessity, if he kills his antagonist, of flying his country, or secreting himself till the next assizes,[15] as he cannot be bailed; and then surrendering himself to a court of justice, there to take his trial for the same, and where he is not certain of escaping a condemnation for murder. Juries have so brought in their verdict, and may do so again. Judges and jurymen are growing every day more serious and severe in this business; and I conceive, it is not three to one, that a man who kills another

---

[14] John Ligonier, 1st Earl Ligonier (1680-1770).
[15] Assizes court handled civil and criminal law.

in a duel, is acquitted of the murder; and even should he be so fortunate as to escape, the state of suspense, and the suffering of his mind in consequence, to a man of feeling, must be great. The bustle, the expence, and danger of a verdict of manslaughter, is bad enough, even if he escapes death.

If *refusing* a challenge is not much in your power, *giving* one is, and the uncertainty of the person (you challenge) accepting it, and not bringing an action against you at law, for so doing, is sufficient to deter a sensible man, from such a step; as you thus put it in the power of your enemy to fine you, and imprison you; and the courts, when such cases are brought before them, seem determined not to spare the challenger, in hopes of abolishing the practice.

If you are reduced to the necessity of giving a challenge, never commit it to writing, but convey it by the friend you have appointed your second; the letter conveying it will be evidence against you in a court of law; your second cannot, as if he convicts you, he convicts himself, which no court will suffer him to do; this evidence he may withhold; but this is a situation I hope you will never be in.

If then you are cautious in giving a challenge, or accepting one; make it a determination never to be a second in such a cause, for the law deems the second as an accessary, makes him equal in guilt with his principal, and if the duelist is convicted of murder, his second will be convicted so also.—Why run your hand into the fire? If you are asked a favor of this sort, rally it off, and refuse it, with saying, "So, you are going to commit murder, and want me to assist you! was I to do this, I should be as mad as yourself."

Economy

My young reader will I hope pardon me, if before we part, I give him a few hints in Economy: the result of my own experience, to which I impute the greatest happiness of my life. In my youth, I ran out as most young men do; spent considerably beyond my income, became involved in debt; was more than once arrested, and continually in fear of bailiffs and a prison. Thus was I on a continual rack, till I took the resolution of lessening my establishment, and living considerably within my income; when I found I was more respected than before, and I was ten times more happy.

We learn this *science* (for Xenophon[16] calls Economy) generally too late to be of any great use to us. Were we to adopt it, at our first outset in life, instead of being poor, and in difficulties at forty, we should be rich, and unembarrassed. Many that are now in distress, had they been frugal in their youth, would be in a state of affluences.

Such is the advantage of living within one's income, that he who had but 500*l.* a year, if he spends but 400*l*, has every year a hundred pounds at command, and may snap his fingers at the world; whereas he who has a 1000*l.* a year, and spends 1200*l.* is every year accumulating a debt of two hundred pounds, and in danger every day of an arrest, and tho' he may be in Parliament, and free from this insult, he is not free from an execution in his house.

The misfortune is, that young men, on coming of age, put perhaps into possession by their guardians, of a good estate, and a

---

[16] Xenophon of Athens (431 BC-354 BC) was an ancient Greek philosopher and a student of Socrates.

considerable sum of money, seldom know its value; for as they draw upon stewards, and bankers, they know not the amount of their wealth, nor do they see it diminish; but consider it in the light of Fortunatus's purse,[17] that replenished itself as fast as it was drawn upon.

I have known young men, at the command of some thousands of pounds, lavish the greater part of it away, before they well knew what they were worth (nay, may have by raising money during their minority half ruined themselves this way,) and spend half their fortune in the first three or four years; and when they have awakened from their golden dream, have found a bailiff at their elbow, and a jail starting them in the face. Then reflection, though to late, has taken place, and to supply their present exigencies, they have found it necessary to mortgage half their estate, and sit down contented to live upon the remaining half.

Listen to me, young man; I have tried it and proved it. The only way to be independent, and free, is to be out of debt, and being out of debt, as the proverb says, "you are out of danger."—What happiness can a man have, who before he leaves his house on a party of pleasure, is obliged to look out and about him, least a Sheriff's officer is lurking to lay hold of him, and lock him up; and who is under the same dread, whilst partaking with his friends in their merriment?—Should what he dreads take place, should he be seized, where is the gentleman—where is that independence and liberty, the pride and boast of Englishmen? A low bred surly fellow and his follower, have got him by the arms, at the suit of his tailor, or his hair-dresser, and is carrying him to prison; because he has not perhaps, twenty pounds, to set himself free.

---

[17] A reference to the German myth about a young man named Fortunatus who received a magical purse that is always replenished with money from the goddess of Fortune.

But admitting, that it does not come to this; he who, through folly, lavishes away half his income, in the first five years of his life, is obliged for the ensuing forty years, if he lives so long, to pinch and deprive himself of those pleasures, and comforts, which he would otherwise have enjoyed.

Let me then remind you of, and recommend you to do that, at first, which you must do at last; namely, sit down, as soon as in possession of your estate or property, consider and estimate its annual value, and arrange your expences accordingly. If your property consists of money in the funds, you are by no means to draw upon, or lessen the principal, but proportion your annual expenditure to, and live upon, the interest. In doing this, you never can be hurt, provided you never run in debt; but refrain from the purchase of anything, 'till you have the money to pay for it.

If your fortune consists in estates, consult with your steward, and learn from him, if the rental, suppose is 1000*l.* a year, how much it will afford you to spend yearly, after you have paid all the necessary out goings and rents, taxes, repairs? And if he tells you 800*l.* content yourself with 700*l.* and form your establishment accordingly; it is better to do this, than run out, and be obliged in a few years, to live upon five hundred pounds a year.*

*To be respectable it is not necessary to live in a certain line of life; a man should give dignity to his situation, and not his situation to him; every man may be considered as the centre of a circle, some of a larger, some of a smaller, and in this light, he is of greater or less importance, according to the character he bears. He who has fewest wants, and is most able to live within himself, is not only the happiest, but the richest man, and is he does not abound in what the world calls *wealth*, he does in *independency*, and it being independence only, that can make us great; by all means confine your expences to your fortune, and determine to live free from debt.—*Principles of Politeness.*

No one, but those who go to market with ready money, know the advantage of so doing. I have done it for more than thirty years. By purchasing cloth, and employing tailors, my suit of cloaths costs me but £1. 15s. which a master-tailor, who gives long credit, would charge 6 or 7*l.* for; this is saving cent. per cent.; but in all things we purchase, 20 per cent. may at times be saved, if the buyer knows what he is about; and this in the expenditure of 500*l.* is 100*l.* of course by not taking credit, a man of 500*l.* a year, can make an appearance equally well with his neighbour, who spends 600*l.* a year, without this attention and care; and so on, in equal proportion. In larger establishments, 5000*l.* will go as far as 6000*l.* which additional 1000*l.* would put this gentleman perfectly at his ease; or it might be laid by for younger children, or be given to support the eldest son when of age.

Lord Chesterfield says, "No one is aware of the advantage of frugality, but those who have tried it. There is scarce a year in a man's life, but a little ready money, may be laid out to advantage; whatever you do therefore, live a good deal within your income, and dread as much taking up money on annuities, &c. before you are of age, as you would of robbing your *banker*; for this is robbing *yourself*."

A few words more on expenditure, and I have done. If you wish to be well respected in the neighbourhood where you live, avoid wrangling, or disputing with your tradesmen, or workmen; with the first, always make a bargain if you can; if not, should you think of yourself imposed on, pay the bill without murmuring, and without deductions, if they will not readily consent to it; and deal with them no more; but don't tell them so, it will answer no good purpose, and only put them out of temper, and induce them to speak ill of you. If you employ another tradesman in their business, they will soon discover the cause of it. Should your wine, your coals, &c. run short of measure, you have only to consider, that such is the nature of trade, that you are not to expect 36 bushels to a chaldron,[18] or 3 gallons to the dozen, and then you will never consider yourself as cheated; you expected short measure, and you are not disappointed.

With the workmen you employ, you must do the same, never expect the day work to commence at six, or that they will keep their time; expect but 10 hours work for the pay of 12, and you will never be disappointed. It is indeed cruel to bear hard upon the pay of a day labourer; consider the time he purloins from you, as so much given him in charity, and shape your donations accordingly. By not living well with the lower class of people, you endanger your fences, your fruit, and your windows.

The great rule is to be *frugal* in *great matters*, and *liberal* in small ones. Sixpence or a shilling, thrown away occasionally, among waiters at inns, hackney-coachmen and chairmen, and the riff-raff of society, conciliates their esteem, and secures their affection.

But, let me refer to a tract of mine, called, *The way to the Rich and Respectable*; a book, which from its great utility, has gone thro' six editions. It will afford many useful hints—price, 4s.

DRESS.

AFTER all, perhaps it may be said, that unless I say something of dress, my system will be yet incomplete; I must not therefore omit making some few observations on this head, it being one of the distinguishing marks of a Gentleman.

To be clean in our person is so necessary to our own comfort and health, that independent of what we owe to others I should think directions on this head almost wholly unnecessary.*

---

[18] A measurement for coal.

*To neglect our dress, is to affront all the female part of our acquaintance. The women in particular, pay an attention to their dress; to neglect therefore yours, will displease them; as it would be tacitly taxing them with vanity, and declaring that you thought dress not worth that respect which everybody else does.—*Principles of Politeness.*

Dress, as trifling as it may appear to a man of understanding, prepossesses on the first appearance which is frequently decisive.— *Principles of Politeness.*

A sensible man dresses as fashionably and well as persons of the best families and best sense; if he exceeds them he is coxcomb; if he dresses worse, he is unpardonable.—*Principles of Politeness.*

When once dressed, think no more of it; shew no fear of discomposing your dress, but let all your motions be as easy and unembarrassed, as if you was at home in your dishabille.—*Principles of Politeness.*

We should in general be so clean as to have no offensive smell about us, not only in our persons, but in our cloaths [clothes]. If we wear our clothes too long without changing them, they will acquire a smell. We should be particularly nice in our feet, our hands, and our hair. Fashionable people scent their cloaths [clothes] with perfumes, but this I call a disagreeable fashion, for Martial says,

Ille qui semper bené *olet,* malé *olet.*

He who always smells *well*, smells *ill*.

It is much better to be extremely cleanly in your person and dress and leave nature to herself, for perfumes are too often used to cover natural disagreeable odours.

A real gentleman is always particularly nice and cleanly about his teeth, the borders and roots of his hair, and the nails of his hands, so as to leave no appearance of dirt.*

*He who is not thoroughly clean in his person, will be offensive to all he converses with. A particular regard to the cleanliness of your mouth, teeth, hands, and nails, is but common decency: a foul mouth and unclean hands are certain marks of vulgarity; the first is the cause of an offensive breath, which nobody can bear, and the last is declarative of dirty work. We may always know a gentleman by the state of his hands and nails; the flesh at the roots should be always kept back, so as to show the semi-circles at the bottom of the nails; the edges of the nails should never be cut down below the ends of the fingers, nor should the tops of the nails be encircled with a black rim; the dirt should be either brushed or picked clean—*Principles of Politeness*.

Then, as to dress, it is proper to look like other gentlemen, never to be in the extreme of the fashion, unless you wish to be considered as a puppy.

Take care to have your clothes made by a fashionable taylor, and not to be the *first out* of the fashion, nor the *last in* it; and let the fashion be what it may, never think of wearing any part of your dress, if it be unbecoming; your glass and your friends will instruct you in this.

The better dressed you are, the more respectable you will appear; but let it be on Horace's[19] plan, *simplex munditiis*, neat, plain, and becoming your rank in life.

He who *pays* a visit should always go better dressed than he who *receives* one, and always more dressed in an *evening* than a *morning*, and when going to meet Ladies than Gentleman. Dress is a compliment we owe to society; you should not shew a remissness therein, unless you would be thought a sloven.

It is the fashion in exalted life now among equals, never to be at home to a morning visitor; nor indeed to any visitor we are

---

[19] Quintus Horatius Flaccus (65 BC-8 BC), known in English as Horace was a Roman poet.

not in the habits of intimacy with; therefore, to refuse admittance to a visitor, you are not disposed to receive, will not be considered rude. At such times, your servant should be directed to say that you are *not at home*. This is in fact no lie, for the expression *not at home*, merely implies that you are not disposed to see company, and is understood in this sense. Of course, if you meet with the same reply when you go to pay a visit, you are not to be offended; unless you had been particularly invited, and you go at the appointed time. For so much do persons of fashion wish to be at their ease, that such ceremonies are introduced, as put them perfectly so.

Indeed, if a superior pays you a visit, it will be a compliment paid him to be seen, if you really are at home, let your dress be what it may; but with equals and inferiors you may do as you please.

The End

Other Books By This Author

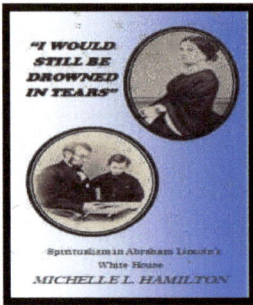

"I Would Still Be Drowned in
Tears": Spiritualism in
Abraham Lincoln's White
House

"My Heart Is In The Cause"
...: The Civil War Diaries of
Private James A. Meyers,
45th PA Volunteers

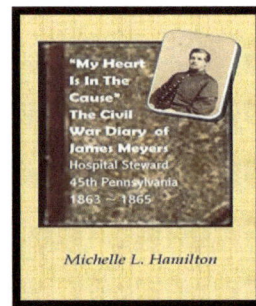

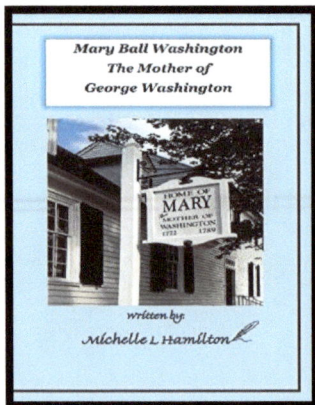

Mary Ball Washington -
Mother of George
Washington"

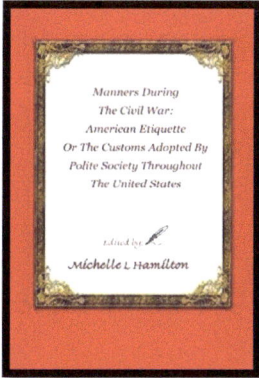

"Manners During the Civil War: American Etiquette, or the Customs Adopted by Polite Society Throughout The United States"

"Civil War Ghosts"

Researched from newspapers of the time

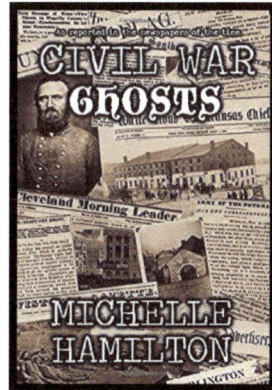

Available on Amazon
Or for an autographed copy
Contact Michelle L. Hamilton
Historywiz1@gmail.com
http://www.michellelhamilton.net/

www.ingramcontent.com/pod-product-compliance
Lightning Source LLC
LaVergne TN
LVHW072329080426
835509LV00033B/144